DESERTS

Troll Associates

DESERTS

by Keith Brandt

Illustrated by James Watling

Troll Associates

Library of Congress Cataloging in Publication Data

Brandt, Keith, (date)
  Deserts.

  Summary: Describes the characteristics of deserts and
the types of plants and animals that live in them.
  1. Deserts—Juvenile literature. [1. Deserts]
I. Watling, James, ill. II. Title.
GB611.B68   1985   910'.02'154   84-8623
ISBN 0-8167-0262-4 (lib. bdg.)
ISBN 0-8167-0263-2 (pbk.)

Listen to the whistling wind! Howling and blowing, it carries clouds of sand into the air. Each tiny grain of sand is a stinging pellet, and there is no shelter in sight. This is a sandstorm in the desert. Unlike other kinds of storms, no rain or sleet falls on the land. There is only the dry, blowing wind, tearing along stretches of sand and rocks.

As the wind lessens and stops, the desert becomes quiet. Overhead, the skies have cleared to a brilliant blue. The sun is blazing. But the storm has written the signs of its fury on the land. Ripples of sand make beautiful patterns across the wide, flat plains. These are the fingerprints left by the wind's movement.

In the distance are giant *dunes*, or hills of

sand. The wind has been at work on the dunes—building them up and tearing them down, constantly shifting the countless grains of sand that make up each dune.

The desert seems a strange and lonely place. But a few hardy plants and animals do live here. And, surprisingly, deserts are fairly common. About one third of the land on Earth is made up of deserts.

If you could travel in a spaceship, circling the globe, it would be easy to see where the Earth's hot, dry deserts are. Seen from the air, they form two belts, which stretch around the middle of the planet. One belt lies to the north of the *equator*—the imaginary line that divides the Earth in half.

In this northern belt, the wide sands of the world's largest desert, the Sahara, stretch across northern Africa. In Asia, the huge Arabian and Gobi deserts cover much of the land. In North America lies another desert —it's the rocky Mojave Desert of the western United States.

In the belt of deserts lying to the south of the equator are the Great Sandy Desert of Australia, and the Kalahari Desert of southern Africa. South America also has many hot, dry deserts. Along this continent's western coast is the driest desert in the world. Not a single drop of rain has ever been recorded there!

11

But these are only the hot deserts of the Earth. Did you know that some deserts are bitterly cold? The Earth's *polar regions*, the land at the North and South Poles, are called *cold deserts*. The air there is so cold that any moisture is quickly frozen. It cannot be used by plants, animals, or people. In this way, the hot and cold deserts are alike: they lack usable water.

Although deserts are widespread over the Earth, it takes a very special sort of plant or animal to live in such a dry climate. The desert's plants and animals have *adapted* to their rugged surroundings. This means they have changed little by little over thousands of years. They now have special ways of gathering the precious water they need to stay alive.

Among the gray and golden sands of the hot, dry deserts, cactus plants dot the plains. These tough plants come in many shapes and sizes. Some are tall and thin. Others are round and short. But all cactuses can store water for long periods of time.

The inside of a cactus is filled with fibers, which soak up and hold rain and dew. And the prickly thorns that cover a cactus protect it from thirsty animals that might just try to bite into its juicy fibers.

After a rare spring rainstorm, the barren desert suddenly changes. It is filled with color. All across the sands, flowers pop up. Even the cactuses are in bloom. But this beautiful sight does not last for long. The seeds of these plants have waited a long time for rain. Now they must quickly flower and form new seeds, before the summer heat stops their growth.

Why is the desert so dry? This seems a puzzling question, especially because so many of the world's deserts are near oceans. But very often, high mountains or high, flat lands called *plateaus* form a barrier between the ocean and the desert. When rain clouds form over the ocean, they drift toward the mountains. They are stopped. Their rain never reaches the desert.

Although the desert gets little rain, rivers and springs sometimes run underground. Where these sources of water rise to the surface, an *oasis* forms. Here, water soaks the mineral-rich desert soil, and many plants grow. Like small islands of lush greenery, oases flourish in a sea of sand.

The animals of the desert are attracted to the oases to quench their thirst and to find food. Some animals do not actually drink water, but get the water they need by eating plants or other animals. In the Arabian Desert, the jackal prowls in search of food. Its North American cousin, the coyote, roams the Mojave Desert of California. If the coyote can't find meat, it will get water by eating plants and nuts.

The best-known desert animal of Africa and Asia is the camel. This strange animal is especially suited to life in the desert. On long legs, it strides across the sand. The wide pads on its feet keep the camel from sinking. No wonder camels have been called "ships of the desert." During a sandstorm, the camel has double protection. Its nostrils are able to close tightly to keep out the stinging grains of sand, and each eye is protected by long eyelashes and three eyelids!

Probably everyone's heard about the camel's ability to skip a meal or two. Its body tissues and the fat in its hump store usable water and food. This lets the camel go for many days without a meal. The camel's rough tongue and lips also help it. Where other animals might be afraid to bite into a cactus, the camel has less trouble—at least most of the time!

21

Great
horned
owl

Cactus wren

Owls, cactus wrens, and roadrunners are a few of the birds that live in the deserts of the southwestern United States. In years of drought—when no rain falls—some birds seem to sense that water and food will be even scarcer than usual. In those years, they do not lay eggs or build nests until the drought is over.

During the day, snakes and lizards hide from the strong, hot sun. As night settles over the desert, they come out from the shelter of rock or cactus in search of food.

Plants and animals are not the only living things in the desert. For thousands of years, people have found ways to survive here.

Common king snake

Roadrunners

23

Chuckwallas

In the Sahara, tribes of *nomads* travel in search of water. These people set up camp wherever they find an oasis. A group of nomads may have as many as 100 families. They are led by one chief. Nomads have very few possessions—for they must travel light. After finding water, they pitch their tents and let their flocks of goats and sheep graze on the desert plants.

When water and food are used up, they must move on to another oasis. Wearing robes to shield themselves from the sun, the nomads break camp and load up their camels. They are ready to move on once again.

In the Gobi Desert of Asia, nomads are traders in addition to being herders. They carry goods to trade from place to place. Over routes that are thousands of years old, long camel caravans make their way over rock, hills, and sand. By day, the nomads must endure the hot sun. But as night settles over the desert, the air becomes cold, and frost may even cover the land. Then, the nomads huddle around a fire for warmth.

Some nomads are hunters. In the Great Sandy Desert of Australia, nomads use their sharp eyes and swift running ability to track down food.

Were the deserts always deserts? Scientists do not think so. The rocks and minerals of the desert soil give us clues about the desert's past. Where salt deposits are now found, there were once lakes and oceans. After they dried up, their salt was left behind.

The desert also has many rich mineral deposits and valuable fields of oil and coal. This clue suggests that long ago, many more trees and plants grew in the desert. After these plants died, it took millions of years for them to break down into coal.

The minerals, oil, and coal of the desert are important resources. The huge amounts of heat and light in the desert may one day provide another source of energy: *solar energy*—which means "power from the sun." Scientists and engineers are at work on ways to best use the desert's resources.

But the future of the desert has another
side. Some fear that the deserts are growing
larger. Some of the land in or near the desert
is now used for farming and grazing.
Scientists think that more than one third of
this land may soon become barren desert.
This would be a serious danger to the people
who live here, for food and water would
become even scarcer than they are now.

Why are the deserts becoming larger?

Partly because there have been many droughts. But the biggest reason is that the desert land and oases have not been used wisely. As more and more nomads abandon lives of travel, the balance of nature is changed. By staying in one place to farm or raise their herds, the settlers quickly use up scanty supplies of water, food, and firewood. The land becomes barren and useless.

But with proper planning, this problem can be solved. In some deserts, beautiful flowers and vegetables now grow. New farming methods have made the land fruitful again. A special type of irrigation and plastic greenhouses, which help hold in moisture, are some of the ways these farmers are renewing the desert land.

For although they are a difficult and challenging place to live, the deserts form a large and strangely beautiful part of the Earth. Their unique plants and animals, their dunes and oases are all a special part of our planet—and the future of the deserts is a part of our own future.